The

Sands
of
Time

SHONA PATERSON

Matador
9 Priory Business Park
Kibworth Beauchamp
Leicestershire LE8 0RX, UK
Tel: (+44) 116 279 2299
Fax: (+44) 116 279 2277
Email: books@troubador.co.uk
Web: www.troubador.co.uk/matador

ISBN 978 1784620 394

British Library Cataloguing in Publication Data.
A catalogue record for this book is available from the British Library.

Typeset in Aldine401 BT Roman by Troubador Publishing Ltd
Printed and bound in the UK by TJ International, Padstow, Cornwall

Matador is an imprint of Troubador Publishing Ltd

The
Sands
of
Time

*For Tracy, Angela, and Christopher,
my wonderful children, and their children.
Also for Robert, my amazing husband, without
whose love and support I would never have
been able to be truly happy again.*

CONTENTS

SADNESS

It's been almost two years now since Mum and Dad died and an overwhelming sadness took over my life. No longer can I call to give them good news or share the bad. I can't remember if I ever told them how much it meant to me to be able to pick up the phone and find them there, or how much I valued the calm assurance of their love and care as I have travelled through this mad and crazy world. I remember well those times when I have called, sharing times of worry or upset, and yet have come away laughing, feeling better, reassured, and in control. How am I to go on without them? All those exciting and good times, the proud times, of children and grandchildren born, their achievements and happy moments. These times were extra special because I could call and share them with my mum and dad. They were always there, at the end of the telephone, when things went wrong: children in hospital, Kytana's accident, and eventually her untimely death ten years later. They understood. They felt my pain and I could feel their love. The distance in miles between us would melt away as I listened to their voices, softly spoken, at my side; and in those moments we shared together on the phone and in my heart, they were there. Now they are gone, both gone, in a final and cruel nine-and-a-half-week sweep of time and I am left alone, like an orphan, feeling lost and vulnerable and scared of a life without them both.

Is it too late to say I'm sorry? I am. I am sorry for every childhood strop I ever had, for every worry I gave them, and for any time I spoke out of turn or in anger. I am sorry for ever being a selfish and hurtful teenager, for pushing the boundaries too far, sometimes leaping right over them and making their life hell. I am truly sorry. As I look through photographs, I remember that lovely day we had at the zoo. It was a great day. I would be about three, going on four, and I had a huge tantrum because I wanted to take the giraffe home. It seems crazy now. I remember Dad giving me a ticking off for spoiling an otherwise lovely day. The photos take pride of place in our house now. They show a happy time, obviously taken before the strop! Yet every time I look at them I feel bad for spoiling that day. I tell myself I was only three, and probably tired and overwhelmed, but I still feel bad about it. I am sorry for being a total nightmare of a teenager and for ever being horrible to my mum and dad. I thought they were trying to control me and I now realise they were just trying to protect me. The irony is that I walked straight into a teenage marriage only to be controlled for the next thirty years by a man who clearly didn't love me a nanometre as much as they did, and who would eventually leave for another woman – as they had predicted all those years ago. You could say I paid the price for that mistake, but I am sorry for the life it took away from us. The only good thing from this time is the gift of my three wonderful children, whom I treasure with every inch of my being, and the grandchildren they have brought into my life.

I regret not having made enough time to spend with my parents. It wasn't easy when they both moved so far away when I was expecting my first child. Had things been different I would have gone to see them more often. Looking back, maybe I should have tried harder then, before child number two came along, and before I moved abroad. I am sorry their few visits to us over these years were not good ones. The clash of personalities between them and my then husband made me tense and unable to relax enough to enjoy their company. I am so sorry for this. Mum and Dad were both so good to us and he was just horrible to them. I don't suppose it would have helped for them to know he wasn't any nicer to me either!

What is good is that we did have some good times before then and again later in life, and it was great that they instantly loved Robert. I was so scared to tell them I had met him, so soon after splitting up with my first husband. When I told Mum over the phone she was so mad with me at first. Then, when she asked us to meet them in Spain so they could check him out, I was pleased – and nervous. It was ridiculous that I would be afraid to tell them – after all I was forty-four! Robert was scared they wouldn't like him but I just knew they would love him as I do. And they did, instantly. That first meeting would lay the foundations of a great phase of our lives together. I am so grateful for that quick shift to happier times. Those thirteen years we were able to share with them provided us with the opportunity to catch up on all the times we had missed over the years. I know how much they looked forward to our visits. The last five years presented another shift in our relationship, as they both needed more and more care while growing older and less able to manage. I am glad we were able to help them live their lives as they wanted, but it wasn't easy. We would arrive to find Mum looking tired and drawn as she selflessly looked after Dad, and yet within hours the change in her, as the burden of responsibility was lifted from her shoulders for that short time, was like the sun rising at dawn. We always left Mum looking happier and healthier than we had found her. I know how much they valued our visits and looked forward to us coming. I cried buckets every time I left them both, knowing that life was hard for them. Too hard, and I was too far away to give them the help they needed and deserved. Eventually I had to respect it was their choice to be together for as long as they could be. Mum and Dad had that kind of love most people only dream of: so close, so obviously very much in love, never a cross word between them, adoring each other as much at the end of life as at the beginning. I know they were both so grateful for the time and help we gave them, but it was something both Robert and I were happy to be able to do. I would have done anything for them.

Hearing their voices and sharing my life with them is something I will always miss. If there is something beyond this life, then they will know that we are okay. Maybe they will already know all the news – maybe they will know before I do – then I really would be the last to know! Or is the end of life just that? Is it that we are all released from knowing anything, or worrying about what happens here? I am a great believer in the theory that, for every good time, there's a bad time. The wise words Dad said to me once, to remember that 'this too will pass', have stayed with me through the years. Dad wisely told me to remember that in good times and bad times the experiences we face today will pass so that nobody ever has all bad times, but it's worth remembering too, when things are going well, not to expect them always to be so, because nobody ever has all good times either, even if it seems that way when we look at others who seem to have it all. The bottom line is that life is ever changing and nothing stays the same. How true! The grandchildren will miss these words of calm and wise advice as much as I will. They too already miss speaking on the phone, and I am sorry there are great-grandchildren they never met.

I have struggled to find a way through it all, to make sense of it, but then the thought came to me that the answer must be in writing. It seems such a natural way forward for me to write, as this reminds me of the happy times Dad and I shared when we would carefully plan my school essays or writing competitions together and it also helps me to continue to remember the good times we all had. I am hoping this book of stories from the past will be a good way to help future generations share in the life of a family they belong to but never got to know, and I dedicate this book in memory of my lovely parents.

As I continue on this journey through life without my mum and dad, I thank them for the love and care they gave to me so freely and generously, although I am not sure I always deserved it. Most of all it gives me great strength to know that the last words we ever said to each other were 'I love you'.

1

NANA AND GRANDDAD ANDERSON

12 Palm Avenue

I loved going to visit my Nana and Granddad Anderson in Newcastle. My memory of their house at 12 Palm Avenue in Fenham was one of huge proportions, so I was surprised recently when my cousin Maureen told me it was a tiny house. Maureen was born in this house and still lives nearby so has revisited since those bygone days. Granddad Anderson died when I was only six, so I don't have too many memories of him other than going to the park where he would push me on the swings and afterwards buy me a packet of Rolos to eat on the bus on the way home. I especially loved New Year's Day when we would all go to Nana and Granddad's for dinner and I would meet up with my cousins Maureen and Elaine. Maureen is the daughter of my dad's (late) younger sister Betty and Uncle Albert. Elaine, who now lives in Canada, is the daughter of my (late) Uncle Les, Dad's older brother and Auntie Kathleen (Kath). We would all have dinner round the kitchen table, then the adults would retire to the living room to chat. Children weren't allowed to listen to adult conversation back then, so we would play in the kitchen, usually under the table, which would become the 'den'. The chairs often became the 'train' or the 'bus' – and always Elaine was in charge, although Maureen was the oldest! I loved these times and we all played together really well. It was the only time we were all together, and I think we all looked forward to it after Christmas. Shortly before it was time to go home we'd be allowed back into the living room and Granddad entertained us with magic tricks. Granddad's brother John was a member of the famous Magic Circle in London and Granddad had learned some of the simpler tricks from him. He always explained how it had been done, and Maureen and Elaine always understood – but I never did! On occasions, we would all stay with our grandparents – not together, but now and again on our own. The first time I stayed with Nana Anderson was after Granddad died. Nana took me to her over-sixties club called the Fenham Evergreens and I always helped with the tea and biscuits. There was never any coffee; no one really drank coffee back then, and if they did they were considered to be extremely posh! When tea was finished we'd all sing along to their signature tune 'The Happy Wanderer' before they left. I still remember the words:

'We shall meet again next week, and have a real good time,
The entertainment's always good, the cup of tea just fine,
Faldereee, falderaaah, faldereee, falderah, ha ha ha ha ha ha
As we go … say cheerio,
We're the Fenham Evergreens!'

After Granddad Anderson died, Nana moved into a high-rise flat in Westgate Road, in the centre of Newcastle. Nana moved into Westgate Court on the seventh floor. It was really quite nice for her as all the people living on that floor were about the same age as herself and widows. They had an agreement to leave their front door open when they were open to visitors and willing to share a cup of tea and a blether. When I was about nine I started going to visit my nana after school on a Friday – not every Friday – just now and again. I would get the bus from the stop outside our school in Whitburn, near Sunderland, to the bus terminus in Newcastle. Nana was always there at the terminus waiting for me, and Mum and Dad would come for me on Sunday night. It wasn't until I was older that I realised that not only was all of this in the days before mobile phones, but also in the days when people didn't have house phones, at least not many people, and certainly not my mum and dad or nana. So I asked myself this: "If I had not been on the bus, how would anyone have known I was missing? Would Nana assume the arrangements had been changed? Or would she go to the police and report me missing?" Certainly, the arrangements were usually made by either letter to home or Nana would phone Mum or Dad at work from a phone box, but they wouldn't be at work over the weekend! Of course this didn't worry me at the time; I was used to looking after myself. My mum started working full-time the day after I started school so I had the key of the house on a string round my neck and would come home and wait for them coming home from work – usually around six in the evening. This isn't allowed anymore now, but it never did me any harm, and it certainly wasn't unusual. Most of the children in the street were the same.

One of the things I didn't like very much, however, was being in the house with Nana when she went to sleep, or when she took what she called 'forty winks'. It was just a wee lie-down on the settee in the afternoon. I was terrified she might die – being so old – and I wouldn't know what to do, so as a precaution I never let her sleep for long before waking her up! Looking back now, she was probably only in her early sixties – and I'm not too far away from that myself now.

The Outside Toilet

It may be hard to believe these days, but when my dad was a little boy, houses didn't have bathrooms – or toilets – honestly! There would be little outbuildings in the yard or garden with a toilet; it was like a small shed with just the toilet and sometimes no washbasin. What's more, there was none of this soft toilet paper. If you were posh there might be what they called 'Izall', a kind of medicated paper that was an excellent substitute for tracing paper. However, most people just used old newspapers and they would be torn or cut into squares and threaded on a piece of string, which would often hang on a nail in the toilet. I can't remember ever living in a house like this, but I do remember my Auntie Betty's house in Gateshead still had this facility right up until I was about ten. I hated going outside to the toilet in the dark

Nana and Granddad Anderson

and into the little 'shed' – it was really creepy, so my cousin
Maureen had to come with me. Maureen is six years older
than me so she always seemed very grown up and I just loved
her, as I do now. She was so kind and patient and she would
never complain about having to take me out in the cold and
dark. "Howay then," she'd say to me in her Geordie accent,
and we'd run out the back. If it were raining, poor Maureen
would be stuck outside telling me to be quick! Anyway, as
these houses with the outside facilities became older and new
houses were built, they were all built with inside toilets and
bathrooms. Some properties would be renovated and Nana

and Granddad Anderson were one of those who received news by letter through the post from the council advising them of the changes. You'd think people would be thrilled for this, but back then, believe it or not, folk were not thrilled, and didn't think it was very hygienic. My nana's comment was typical of the general thought: "Uuugh, doing the toilet in the house, that's disgusting!"

Nana Anderson's Hat and Coat Trick

Nana Anderson had a coat-and-hat stand in the hallway of her house. I was always bemused by the fact that she always put on her hat before answering the door. Thinking it must be some kind of old-fashioned politeness, I asked her why she did it. "Well," she said. "If it's someone I want to see I say I've just come in, and if it's someone I don't want to see, I'm just on my way out!" What a great idea!

2

GRANNY AND GRANDDAD JORDAN

50 Stenhouse Place East

We all went to stay with Granny and Granddad Jordan for Christmas, travelling up on the train *The Flying Scotsman* on Christmas Eve. It was always dark when we arrived at Waverley Station and we'd take one of the big black taxi cabs to Granny and Granddad's house at 50 Stenhouse Place East in Edinburgh. It was where Mum grew up and she always referred to it as 'home' no matter where we lived. I loved travelling through the bustling Princess Street at night and loved seeing the bright lights of the city as we passed through it. Edinburgh was special, and I find myself thinking of it as 'home' now too. We'd all have Christmas there together, and of all the presents I probably got I can only remember ever really looking forward to a 'selection box' and the *Oor Wullie* annual, which I would read all morning. Mum and Gran fussed about in the small kitchen making Christmas dinner and we'd all have a great time. At night, Granddad always arranged a visit to the pantomime in town, arriving by taxi, but coming back by bus. I loved it. When we arrived home I was always tired and went straight to bed – a little 'put-me-up' folding bed which was put in Mum and Dad's bedroom. Granny and Granddad lived in a block of four flats. Their flat was on the ground floor, and I loved being all on the same level. As I lay in bed I could hear the chatter and laughter from the living room and it made me feel very safe.

During the summer I went to stay with them for much longer. We'd come up by train again and Mum and Dad would go back home, and then come back for me some weeks later. I had lots of friends there and it was great. There weren't many friends in child terms where I lived then – even my best friend Pam was a bit of a distance away –but here in Edinburgh there were children my age all round the Place East. Catherine Drummond lived opposite my gran and granddad with her brothers and sisters, Patricia, Alex, Tommy and Diane. Catherine's mum and dad worked and she had to look after her younger brothers and sisters so we all played in their 'back green' – the communal space behind the houses – together. We were often joined by my other friend Grace, who lived in the top flat beside the bus stop at the cross. Favourite 'stomping grounds' were the zoo, where a hole in the fence allowed us free access, and we also loved time playing in Saughton Park. Half of Mum and Dad's ashes lie there now in one of the beautiful gardens under a large willow tree. It was a favourite place for them too.

When it was the end of the holidays, and I had to go home again, Granddad organised a taxi to take us back to Waverley Station and my friends all gathered to say goodbye, running behind the taxi waving me off to the end of the street as I kneeled on the back seat of the taxi waving back!

Granddad Jordan and Telephones

When I was young nobody had telephones in the home. There were no landlines and no mobile phones. There were public telephone boxes and I remember having to pick up the phone, put your money in a slot, and dial the number. If someone answered, you pressed button A and you would be connected, and if you pressed button B your money was returned if there was no reply. I would sometimes use the phone box to phone my mum at work but eventually, through the passage of time, people started to get phones installed in their homes. As Mum and Dad both had well-paid jobs they considered this option, so Nana and Granddad Jordan, who both lived 200 miles away, could phone them if they needed something, or Nana Anderson, living twenty miles away, could also call them if she needed to. Mum ran the idea past Granddad Jordan when he next called her at work. "Phone?" he repeated with a puzzled tone. "They are just for businesses, not for houses, it's just a fad, it'll never catch on!" I wonder what he would make of our technology now?

Crisps and Nuts

After Granddad Jordan died Mum and Dad made sure

Granny Jordan spent some time with them in Hertfordshire. They would drive up to Edinburgh, spend a few days there, and bring Granny back to spend a week or two with them. Trying to make her stay as nice as possible, they took her out for a run in the car, often stopping off at little country pubs for lunch or a drink. After a while Granny found a couple of favourite stops, one being a regular of Mum and Dad's – The King William, or 'The Willie' as it was affectionately known – where she had come to know many of the regulars and people who already knew Mum and Dad. They would always politely stop and ask how she was and have a chat. Knowing how much she enjoyed going there, my dad asked her if she'd like to call in on the way home from their run out to the country. "Only if I can pay for the drinks," she replied, with some determination. "It's okay," said Dad, "this is your treat, you don't need to pay." Granny looked at Dad and with steely determination repeated her 'condition'. "Only if I can pay for the drinks." My dad reluctantly agreed, knowing that it wouldn't cost too much. After all, they'd already been out for lunch and drinks; this was a little extra to the normal routine. As always they found a comfortable corner, and while Granny was taking off her coat and getting settled, a couple of regulars came in with their ageing parents and they all began chatting. "What will you have?" asked Granny, adding, "It's my treat today," and, looking at my dad, told him to take a note. "I'll get these," Dad said, trying to save her from the shock of the expense of a 'round', but the protests were clear and loud and Dad dutifully took the orders. "Gin?" asked Granny. "Have a double." And so it went on.

"You'll go to be bar?" Granny whispered to Dad, as she slipped a crumpled note into Dad's trouser pocket, adding, "and get everybody crisps and nuts with the change. "When Dad went to the bar and took out the crumpled note, he noticed it was a £1 note! The round came to more than £15 but he graciously thanked Granny and never said a word!

Television

Granny Jordan was a very proud Scot and loved all things Scottish. She was especially fond of a television programme called *The White Heather Club* which featured Scottish country dancing and old musical acts such as The Alexander Brothers, who sang all the old favourite Scottish songs wearing kilts and playing the accordion. It was not until the 1970s that colour television sets became available. Up until then shows had all been in black and white and Mum and Dad were some of the first people I knew to purchase a colour television. When they asked Granny Jordan whether she might like one, so she could watch her favourite programmes, she gave it little thought before answering, "Och no, I think I prefer the black and white – it's more natural!"

The Medieval Banquet

Medieval Banquets were all the rage in the '70s. They were a bit like the 'all you can eat' deals we get now, but hosted in an ancient past setting – a sort of 'theme'. They were great deals for those who could eat, with every kind of meat you could think of – suckling pig on a spit, roast beef, chicken, salmon, lobster – and all the vegetables and side dishes you could think of. I wouldn't describe it as 'cheap' but for a deal where you could help yourself to whatever, it was pretty good value. Mum and Dad thought it would be a good idea to take Granny to one, as she had a good appetite and would probably not treat herself normally to the many expensive types of meat or fish on offer. After being shown to their seats and having watched some 'entertainment', they all made their

Granny and Granddad Jordan

way to the banqueting table. Mum had a plate full of duck and pheasant and other such things. Dad went for the salmon and fish selection. When Granny came back to the table she had a plate full of potatoes! "That's a lot of potatoes," Dad remarked, then asked, "why didn't you get some meat?" Granny just looked at Dad. "Can you have whatever you like?" she asked. "Yes," Dad replied with encouragement. "Well I like tatties!" Recalling the event, Dad remarked, "I can't believe I've paid the price of a three-course meal for a plate of spuds!"

3

MUM AND DAD

Stories

It was always my dad who would read the bedtime story before I went off to sleep, and I loved them. I had my favourites, with one in particular becoming my special favourite. It was about a teeny-weeny house, and everything was teeny-weeny. One day, when Dad couldn't find the book about the teeny-weeny house, I asked him to make up a story but he said he would need time to think about it, so we just chatted, and he quizzed me about what kind of story I would like. I think I said I'd like something about teeny-weeny things! Dad was a civil servant in a very busy office, and he didn't drive so he had to leave quite early in the morning as he worked quite far away from our home, and he was home quite late. The next night when I asked him what story he had prepared for bedtime he told me he hadn't had any time that day. I was shocked and asked him what he had been doing all day!

The Missed Chance of Fame and Fortune

When I was little, everyone I knew had a piano in his or her house. My nana and granddad had a piano and we had a piano. I guess in the days before television people got together to make their own entertainment. My dad and my Uncle Les were good pianists and they would gather at Nana's house with friends who often played guitar, and they'd all have a good singsong. I just loved hearing my dad play and he tried to teach me. I thought it was naff, and all I wanted to do then was go out and play, something I regret now. As television became more popular, people got together less for these singsongs and instead spent time watching the stars of the day doing the same on television. One of the programmes Mum and I used to watch was one where there was a man playing the piano and a lady singing. I loved singing so I suggested that Dad and I go on television; he could play the piano and I could sing. I never did get an answer because Dad couldn't stop laughing long enough to give me one.

Driving lessons

When I was about twelve, my mum and dad started to take driving lessons. Mum did really well after a number of lessons and passed first time. Dad on the other hand didn't. For someone who had flown planes and captained speedboats, you'd think a car would come naturally – it didn't. I guess the thing about boats and planes is the lack of other boats and planes in the area while navigating, unlike cars that become part of the traffic. Dad told me of one early lesson when the instructor had wanted him to turn left. "Look in your mirror and start slowing down now," he told Dad. "Assess the traffic flow behind you, check your side mirrors, and signal you are about to turn." Dad was still assessing the traffic and trying to find the right lever to signal, but by the time he did all that they had passed the road they needed to go down! Dad was obviously a bit of a worry on the road to the instructor because his next lesson was at a disused airfield. This time it was to practice reverse. Again, Dad followed the instructions to look in the mirror, assess his place on the road, and consider the manoeuvre. So there Dad was, looking in the rear-view mirror, instructor turned round to watch the area behind the car, as the car shot forward! He'd forgot to put it in reverse. After several disastrous lessons, the instructor told Dad that some people were just never meant to drive, and the lessons ended, for good.

Mum's the Word!

When we lived at Hawthorn Terrace, Dad worked for Her Majesty's Revenue and Customs Office in Longbenton, an area of Newcastle. As he didn't drive, he travelled home by train and bus and would never be home too early. Mum by now was working at the Roker Hotel in Sunderland as Head Receptionist and worked shifts, so she would often be away to work before Dad got home, which of course meant that I came home when no one was in. But it was expected that Dad would be in before half past six at the latest. Occasionally, in bad weather this arrangement fell short of the expected and it sometimes failed completely at times when Dad fell asleep on the train or bus and ended up in South Shields! On one particularly foggy night, his bus broke down and he was really late. When he was very late, he would look at the time and apologise, adding, "Don't tell your Mam." It was an arrangement that suited me fine in the summer months of the long light nights. No longer was the rule to come home when the streetlights came on, because they didn't, and I very often lost track of time. Many nights I would be on my own, just walking along the promenade watching the waves or examining rock pools for baby crabs. So when I eventually ventured home, a worried Dad would ask, "Where have you been?" and "Look at the time!" Then, "You'd better get washed and ready for bed," and then, "do you want some milk and something to eat?" "Yes Dad, sorry Dad." He would smile at me and shake his head. "I was worried about you," then, "where were you?" "Ah, just down at the beach," I would sigh, as I climbed the stairs and, "sorry Dad, I didn't realise it was so late." "Okay pet," he'd say, then, "don't tell your Mam!"

Breakfast in Bed

One Sunday morning, when I was about thirteen, I decided I would make breakfast for Mum and Dad as a surprise. I was up much earlier than them on a Sunday, so waited until I could hear signs of them getting up before going in the room with the tray. I carefully prepared breakfast as they liked it, heated teapot cups and saucers, milk jug but no sugar. I put little plates on the tray and boiled the kettle. I reached up for the marmalade in the cupboard, Dad's favourite, and took the butter out of the fridge to soften a little. Butter didn't come in tubs that could be spread straight from the fridge in those days; it came in blocks that were always rock-hard when you took them out of the fridge. Checking everything was in place, I sat listening, patiently waiting, ready for the 'sign'. I waited and waited, boiled the kettle several times, and waited some more. Eventually, I heard a noise and as quick as a flash the plan was put into action. Kettle boiled, teapot warmed, toast on. Then tea made, toast spread with marmalade for Dad and some with just butter for Mum, all carefully prepared on the tray, and a little vase from the hall with a plastic flower in it for added value! I carefully carried the tray along the long hallway to their room and opened the door using my elbow, manoeuvring the tray round so I wouldn't spill or drop anything. It was heavy. I then quietly walked into the room. And … they were both fast asleep! Hell! What was I going to do now? Should I wake them up? I decided no, they really looked forward to their Sunday lie-in. I thought a minute or two, then decided that they were probably due to wake up soon so I carefully laid the tray down on the floor by Dad's side of the bed. It must have been about twenty minutes later or so when I heard a sign alright! It came in an almighty clatter, followed by "Bloody Hell!" It was Dad's voice, then the next sounds were *thump, thump, thump, thump, thump* as he hopped all the way up the long hallway to the bathroom to wash the marmalade and butter off his foot! I think it was probably the last time I brought them breakfast in bed, and to tell you the truth I think my dad was quite glad!

Holidays

After I left home, Mum and Dad spent many holidays abroad and this incident in particular always makes me smile …

Mum and Dad loved their time holidaying in Fuengirola, Spain, staying at the same apartment they rented from someone who lived in the UK. They had the same 'packing up and leaving' routine every time they went, with the same taxi driver knocking at the back door they would leave from. The cases would be at the back door, keys and bags ready, with the front door firmly locked, all ready to go. On one occasion the taxi arrived early and a new taxi driver knocked at the front door. Unfortunately they were caught off-guard, and in the panic with Mum shouting from upstairs that the taxi had arrived, Dad had to find the keys to open the front door and then quickly move the cases and bags from the back door to the front, remembering then to lock the back door. Mum came running downstairs as the suitcases and bags were being stacked in the taxi and they quickly locked up the front door. The whole experience had taken them by surprise and Mum worried that Dad may have forgotten something in the rush. "Tickets, passports, keys of the apartment?"

Mum asked as Dad checked all were present. "Did you lock the back door, are the windows closed, is the cooker off?" All to which Dad confidently responded, "Yes." They were in the departure lounge of the airport when Mum gave out a shriek. Looking down at Dad's feet, she noticed he still had his slippers on!

Retirement

Dad had not been looking forward to retiring. He didn't have any hobbies, and would reject any ideas of suddenly adopting one. I called him one day, a few weeks after he had retired, to see how he was coping. "Oh, I'm great," he said, and added, "it's your mum who seems to have the problem." I was curious; Mum was more than ten years younger and still working at that time. "What's the problem?" I asked. "Well," explained Dad. "I was lying here on the couch just the other day and your mum was upstairs cleaning when there was a knock at the door. I shouted up to her 'that's the door' and she shouted back for me to answer it. So I shouted back 'I'm retired mate'." Then he added, "She's just not getting the hang of it at all!" Dad had a great sense of humour and he would often wind my mum up. He once told me, in Mum's presence, that she was argumentative. "No I'm not," she snapped. Dad turned to me, winked, then added, "See what I mean?"

Mum and Shopping

Mum loved shopping, and she loved food – not that she ate that much. But she loved shopping for food and when she wasn't doing that she would be buying recipe books – she had hundreds of them! Her cupboards and freezer were always stacked with foodstuff, and over the years I am certain that some of the food she had stored was older than me! When she became a little less confident about driving and going out shopping, she would look forward to Robert and I visiting so we could take her to the supermarket. It's something we dreaded as it was a test of endurance. Mum wouldn't be happy unless she had scrutinised every tin or packet on the shelves, only to discard them later. It was not unusual for us to be in the supermarket for more than four hours, as Mum couldn't move very fast. As Dad became less steady on his feet, Mum would want me to stay with him, and poor Robert would be the one asked to take her shopping. They could be away for five or six hours, as Mum visited more than one supermarket and market stall, often going through the checkout with two shopping trolleys stacked full of food. If I asked when she intended eating all of this food and reminded her of 'use-by' dates, Mum would dismiss such dates as 'a load of rubbish'. It's a miracle of science they never experienced food poisoning. Mum loved lilies, so Robert or I found time to sneak back to the shop and buy her a bouquet while we were there, and she just loved it! However, crazy as we might have found it, Mum loved these little outings, even if it meant she was so exhausted she spent much of the next day in bed.

As Mum became less able to do her own shopping, one of the ways we were able to help and allow them to stay in their own home was to organise her internet shopping so she could get her groceries delivered. From what I understand, this obsession with food storing was not that unusual, and seems to stem from growing up during the Second World War when food was rationed. Mum was seven when war was declared and it lasted six years but I think rationing probably went on about another year after that as things gradually got back to normal again. When Robert and I went to visit, Mum always had a clipboard waiting with two columns. One column would list jobs for Robert to do while we were there, like fixing a leaky tap or clearing out a gutter, and one column would list jobs for me, like washing the windows or the blinds. There was always more shopping to various places for the 'offers' she had seen from fliers which had been delivered through the letterbox. This took up some time for us but was also quite a good opportunity to take some time out to a café somewhere for a coffee. It was the only break we had and it was very welcome. As Robert and I were both working, our visits were often short but busy, as we made our way through the lists compiled on the clipboard. After one such visit when we were making our exit to head home again, Dad called to Mum, "That's the whirlwind away." I laughed, knowing all too well what he meant. "Is that what it's like for you?" I joked, and Mum said, "Well, let's put it this way, I couldn't be doing with it every fortnight!" I think these short visits exhausted them simply watching us just

Dad on the Piano

as much as it exhausted us, and we laughed and cried as we then made the 500-mile journey home again knowing life would be hard for them without us.

Modern Technology

Since Mum and Dad retired from work, and old familiar systems were replaced by new technology, procedures once simple now became complicated and difficult for them. Mum was constantly exasperated by the lengthy processes in simply making a telephone call to a company or to her bank for information. Once, when one such call would have taken less than five minutes, it seemed to take at least twice that

My mum

time just to get through to the person or department she wanted. "If you are an existing customer, please key in your account number by pressing the digits on your telephone keypad," then, "if you are calling about x Key 1... if you are calling about xx Key 2," and so on. Then there would be 'security questions' such as "what was your mother's maiden name?" This always amused my dad, who rightly observed that in many of the little villages in rural communities everybody would know your mother's maiden name. Of course, in some cases you could choose what your security questions would be or even choose a password you would remember, and it was with this freedom of choice that Mum chose the word 'Trixie', our old family dog, long since passed. On one occasion, when Mum was making one of these calls, the event had taken more than twenty minutes, and when Mum was still not through to the department she needed to speak to, Dad began to take particular interest. Listening to Mum answering question after question, 'First line of your address, mother's maiden name, previous address, time at last address, customer number, all other accounts, dates, times' etc., he called to her, "What do they need all this information for?" He shook his head and, turning to Robert and me, said, "It's ridiculous, all your mother wants to know is what her balance is?" We agreed. Listening to Mum sat at the dining table, totally fed up with the length of time she'd been on the phone, we heard her say "Trixie."

"Bloody hell," said Dad, exasperated. "They even want to know the dog's name now!" This eventually got Mum through to the person she wanted to speak to but she had to get us all to stop laughing first so she could hear!

4

FRIENDS AND FAMILY

Pam

When we moved from 72 Dovedale Road, in Seaburn, to 10 Hawthorn Terrace, in Whitburn, I had to move school. I had just turned nine on 10 August 1963 and actually looked forward to starting a new school. I will never forget my mum taking me to meet the headmaster and then being led to the class I would join. When I walked in the room the headmaster told everyone who I was, and a little pixie of a girl turned to me and, smiling, asked, "Will you be my friend?" I smiled, nodded, and said, "Yes." Pam was one of those tiny wee girls, with small features and a small build. She had really short hair, which framed her face, and she had a big smile. Fifty years on, Pam and I are still friends, best friends. Nothing much has changed, except she is taller than me now and her hair is long. One day at school, not long after I started, a gymnastic group from another school came to give a display, and Pam and I were amazed at this. Afterwards, every playtime or spare minute we had we would practice out on the school field, and after school we had tricks and ideas to try out when we got home. One of the things we did was to do a handstand against the wall and gradually move our hands further back so we would go further over, hitting the wall with our feet, lower and lower down. Eventually we would try it out on the sofa and kick back again in the living room. My mum would go mad at this disruption, and she would get really fed up seeing me upside down more than standing up! After one practice session with Pam in our house, we crashed into the piano and a little ornamental donkey wearing a sombrero fell and smashed into pieces. My mum went nuts and thereafter Pam and I were banned from gymnastics in the house. We later joined our school gymnastic club and after that another. Gymnastics would soon take over our lives, training every day, competitions, displays, and even television appearances. The training became intense as the level of competition rose to great heights. I had to leave when my dad's job meant us moving to Scotland, but Pam continued and went on to compete in the Olympics and was a real star!

Many years later, Pam is still someone I could trust my life with! She has been a huge support to me through the years. She is like the sister I never had and I love her. I remember one time she said she hoped we would still be friends when we were pensioners and there's no reason to doubt that will happen! Robert and I visit her and her husband Dave when we can, and they come to see us from time to time. We always have a great laugh when we get together. Pam is so funny. We were always in trouble at school for mucking about and giggling – nothing has changed!

Lesley

When I was about ten, I had a friend who lived along the road from us in Glaisdale Drive near Hawthorne Terrace, where we lived. Her name was Lesley and her dad was a captain in the Territorial Army. Lesley was horse-mad at a time when I was very much gymnastics-mad and I suppose the difference in interests could have been a problem, but instead it proved to be quite the opposite. At the weekends, when I didn't have exhibitions or competitions, I would go round to see Lesley and we would inevitably play at 'horses'. Lesley would set up a makeshift gymkhana in her back garden using old bins, brooms, boxes, steps, and anything else that could be jumped over. We would each take it in turn to go round the garden, Lesley jumping, throwing her head back like a horse, and giving the occasional *neigh*. I would navigate the obstacles by cartwheels, walkovers, and backflips, as well as a few leaps and jumps. We must have looked like a pair of nutters! In the afternoon we watched the racing on television. We would each pick a horse to win the race and then see who won. Neither of us ever did! Of course we never even considered that we were 'betting' and I can just hear all those involved in social service and child welfare groaning at the thought of exposing vulnerable children to the evils of gambling, but I can tell you it had a very sound effect. There would have been no way, in later years, that I would have actually put money on a race, well knowing it would be money thrown away. Some months later we actually succeeded in securing a weekend job down at the beach and local stables leading beach ponies along the sands for rides by tourists. Seaburn was quite a popular place, and the sand is as lovely now as it was back then. Lesley and I would arrive at the stables, groom the horses, feed and water and saddle them, then ride down to the place where the man would set up. After the day ended we would take them back to the stables, muck them out, and feed and water our 'own pony', before heading home. We were awarded with a shilling or ten pence as it is now. It wasn't much money then but we would have done it for nothing. I usually spent my money on the trampolines on the way home.

Anne

I met Anne in Africa, when I lived in Zambia, where my son Christopher (Chris) was born in 1980. Anne was also from Scotland and she lived next door but one from me. She had a daughter, Gail, and a son, Glen, who was a year older than my Chris. Chris and Glen were good friends and Anne and I were good friends too. We shared both happy and difficult times together and when it came that we would both leave Zambia, Anne and her family headed off to America a short time before I returned to Scotland. Over the years we kept in touch and when Anne came back to Scotland occasionally to visit her mum and dad, Jean and George, we would always catch up. Jean and George were lovely people, so in between Anne's visits to them I would call occasionally to make sure they were well. If there was anything I could have done to help them I would have, but they always said they were fine, and I think they were. Robert came with me when Anne was home after her dad died, and it was good for them to meet and we had a lovely day with them. Anne and I share a special friendship because Anne was also an only child like me. Anne had married young too, with not so happy outcomes, and her mum and dad had worried about her, like mine. She lived abroad and didn't see her mum and dad much, and as they became older and less capable she suffered the same challenges as I have, but in Anne's case her travelling meant round trips of thousands of miles, not hundreds. We each understood the worry, and often the guilt, about living so far away. As Anne's parents have both since passed, we have spent many hours on the phone looking back, sharing laughter and tears, but always we end with laughter, and it is so good to have a friend like Anne. Anne lives in Ireland now, near Gail and her family, but Glen still lives in America. It's hard for Anne having a son who lives so far away and she misses him dreadfully. I understand how she feels. We keep in touch a lot and visit each other when we can. Anne is a true friend.

Pop

When I met Robert I was forty-four and he had turned forty-five just three months earlier. I was nervous about meeting his mum and dad but they couldn't have been lovelier to me. I always called Robert's dad Pop, which is what his grandchildren called him, but when he phoned our house, right from the start he'd say, "Hello Shona, it's Pop here," so that's what I called him. Robert and his mum were very alike in looks and personality and we hit it off right away. She had a great sense of humour and although she sadly passed away less than two years after Robert and I met, I will always remember her telling me she was so pleased Robert had met someone as lovely as me. Isn't that a lovely thing to say? She also asked me to look after him and take care of him, something I was happy to reassure her of. Robert was one of six children then, three sisters, Audrey, Evelyn, and Maureen, and two brothers, Alan and Malcolm. They were all so welcoming to me in those early days and to this day we get on well and I enjoy their company. Audrey died about a year after Robert's mum, Jeanie, after a fairly short illness, and that left only Robert and I living near his dad and brother Malcolm, who lived together then. Evelyn and Maureen were in Aberdeen then and still live there today, and Alan lives in Spain. Eventually Malcolm left home too, to live in Aberdeen, and that meant only Robert and I living near to Pop, except for grandchildren. We would often visit and see how he was getting on, and when he was still driving, he would visit us too. He still had a couple of gardening jobs and loved growing dahlias which he would earn prizes for in competitions. As time went on, he stopped growing the dahlias; he gave up his gardening jobs and then the car. We noticed he would often be forgetful and this sometimes led to misunderstandings when he told the others he never saw us; of course we had been there often. We always brought him to our house on Boxing Day, as he spent Christmas Day with one of his grandchildren who lived nearby, and he never remembered having been there the year before – much to the amusement of others. "You'd think Robert would get the bottle out at Christmas," he said to my daughter Angela one year, and she reminded him he'd had about four whiskies already. He always said, "Well this is my first time at your house in Menstrie," every year he came! Pop loved telling people about his National Service, and as time progressed we'd hear the same stories at least three times during the same visit, but we just smiled as though we'd never heard them before. As with my mum and dad, the care Pop needed increased. Unlike my mum and dad, where the help with them was physical, Pop was suffering from dementia and this was very difficult to manage. Robert and I had a hard task looking after them all, both keeping full-time jobs and fitting in journeys down south too. Increasingly Pop's dementia became worse and when he asked me one day, "Shona, do you see much of Robert these days?" I laughed. Robert was standing beside me. It was incredible that while lots of memories were becoming muddled and confused, he always knew who I was. As his level of dementia increased so did our worry in his vulnerability, but when we reminded him about making sure the door was locked, or not to put newspapers near the gas fire, or offered to help with the housework, he would look at us as though we were mad. "I might be old," he said once, quite sharply, "but I'm not bloody senile." Sadly, he was, and soon we had to make late-night journeys to make sure the door was locked and newspapers were not stacked up too near the gas fire. We tried to have him assessed to get him into care but these things take far too long and, meanwhile, it was becoming clear he was either forgetting to eat, or ate everything to hand, including whole packets of biscuits and cakes. I would make our dinner and keep some back and take it over to him at night. One day I made mince and potatoes and took it over. "That's nice," he said, smiling, "but I don't usually have mince and tatties for breakfast." It was then we realised he was now completely unsure whether it was day or night. We couldn't even be sure, when we checked that the door was locked at night, that he wouldn't venture out again in the early hours. He was confused and vulnerable and we worried constantly about him. When Robert and his sisters eventually found a good care home, and it was agreed he would have a place there, it was a huge relief, mixed in with sadness that this had to happen at all; but his general appearance and health vastly improved for a while, and we realised we had really done the best for him under the circumstances. Our relief was short lived, however, as a few months later he became susceptible to infections and his health took a dip. At a time when I had to go down south to look after my dad, while Mum was in hospital for a heart operation, Pop took another nasty infection, and Robert had to stay at home. The day after I came home, Robert called when I was out with my daughter Tracy to say his dad was much better and in good spirits, so he would go to work for a while. It was a great relief. Tracy and I went for a coffee and, as we were about to leave, Robert called again. This time, his voice was shaky: "Shona, Dad's taken a turn for the worse, we need to get over to the home." I took Tracy home quickly and rushed over to get Robert, and we made our way to the home. Robert's son David arrived to visit soon after, and while the three of us were there by his side, holding hands and talking to him, he slipped away peacefully, and the tears just flowed. It was Sunday 15 April and the sun was shining, but it was raining in our hearts. At his funeral I read a poem about rainbows.

My Wonderful Family

It would be wrong not to include something about my life now, although I think this belongs in another book, one I hope someone will write in later years and carry on the stories. I will be sixty this year! Oh my God that sounds so old. I only feel about thirty-seven. It's hard to believe that life goes on so quickly, almost like a tornado, gathering with it experiences both good and bad and stories like the ones in this book, all whooshed up together gathering strength and speed. I have spent my early life as an only child, spending a lot of time on my own, with parents who worked a lot, and it made me independent and capable. There were always long periods of quiet. How different it is from life now! I have three wonderful children, three great stepchildren, and the most fantastic husband in the world, and together we have twelve grandchildren; some would say eleven but I still count Kytana, the granddaughter we lost. Life is never quiet and there have been more dramas than I care to remember. There has been laughter and tears and some things best left forgotten! My eldest daughter Tracy was born in Falkirk on 26 March 1975, then along came Angela, who was born in Stirling on 23 August 1977; and Christopher was born in Zambia on 14 October 1980. There are a lot of stories there!!! They are all parents themselves now, with Jordan (Tracy's son) born on 9 August 1994; Kytana born on 23 August 1996 and Aron born 3 May 2005 (Chris's kids); and then there's Jamie-Leigh, Chris's stepdaughter, who was born on 7 May (same day as Dale) but two years earlier in 2004. Ryan was born on 8 January 1997, Kerrie 17 November 1999; Dale 7 May 2006 and Jay 12 November 2013 (all to mum Angela). My stepchildren are all boys: Steven, born on 27 September 1973, David, born on 28 March 1979, and Craig, born on 11 June 1984. Steven has two daughters: Monique, born on 24 January 2001, and Rebecca, born on 29 October 2006. David has two sons: Logan, born 1 July 2010, and Aiden, born 9 November 2012. Together they have gathered a host of ex-partners between them, such is modern life now, and at the moment only my Chris and Robert's David are married. Chris married on my birthday, 10 August last year (2013), to Kareen, Jamie-Leigh's mum, and David is married to Alison. They've been married since 30 April 2005. Tracy's single and Angela's fiancé is Greig. Only Craig doesn't have any children yet (at least none that we know about!), and his girlfriend is Gillian, who has a little boy, but we have yet to meet her! Steven is the only one on his own at the moment. So you see, we have a full and busy life, and you will see why I say these stories belong to another book – or even books!!!

Robert and I met on 17 July 1999 and we were married

on 1 March 2003 in Tobago. There is an old and ancient saying: '*You must first experience the bad to truly appreciate the good*'. This has certainly been true for Robert and I. Robert is my rock, he is the most wonderful husband in the world, and I love him dearly. He's ruggedly handsome, funny, strong, gentle, loving, and caring. He worries about me and protects me. He listens to me and encourages me, he unselfishly puts me first always and without hesitation. He is always there for me, ready with a hug, and sometimes to wipe away a tear. We laugh together, cry together, and love together. I would be lost without him. He is my hero. It's true to say that without him and my kids I don't know how I would have got through these past couple of years. Together they have supported me, loved me, and given me strength. My amazing family!

5

SAYING GOODBYE

Saying goodbye has to be the hardest thing to do. Saying goodbye to Dad then Mum has torn me apart. The family had for years been trying to persuade Mum and Dad to move back up to Scotland to be near to us but Mum very firmly dug her heels in and resisted all attempts at persuading them to move. We couldn't understand why, in the twilight of their lives, they wouldn't want to be near the family for the extra support they would come to need. Mum always said, "When something happens to one of us, then that's the time." So we all gave up trying to persuade them eventually, and suddenly I understood. Their home was a sanctuary. It was a place of peace and safety – it was their home, a legacy of their happy times together. This is where they wanted to be, in their own place with each other for as long as they could, with their own routines and their own things around them. The price in achieving this, however, became great. Robert and I gradually increased the number of visits, travelling the 900-mile round trip to a point where we were going down every two weeks. I arranged for their shopping online. Mum would phone her order to me and I would do the internet shop online, which would keep them going in between trips. Our visits were busy ones. Mum had her clipboard with jobs for Robert and jobs for me – and bits of shopping they needed we couldn't get from the supermarket. When we weren't there, neighbours kept an eye out for them and telephoned if something was wrong. Dad was now becoming very frail and spent very little time out of bed, helped over the last few months by nurses who came in to see him for a few minutes twice a day. Of course I worried endlessly, and when Mum had to go into hospital to have a minor heart operation, I had to take time off work to look after Dad then Mum when she came home. It was the start of an incredibly worrying time which would last for several months. Tracy was then admitted to hospital in Scotland to have a difficult operation on an oesophageal pouch. It would be necessary to collapse one of her lungs to enable them to reach the offending pouch. The day after her operation, her lung had not re-inflated and her second lung collapsed. She was rushed into intensive care and we were called to her bedside as she struggled to breathe with the help of apparatus. It was every parent's nightmare. I was tortured watching her struggle, terrified of losing her. It was a terrible time. Eventually there were signs of improvement but she remained in intensive care for three weeks. Then Dad had to go back into hospital to have some investigations carried out on his oesophageal pouch. It was a while before we could go back down again, with Tracy so ill and us having taken so much time off work, but we made a short visit for Mum's eightieth birthday and took her in to see Dad in hospital. Her own ill health had meant she couldn't go and visit so this, she said later, was the best present she could have wished for. I could see how much this meant to her so, after some searching, discovered a local taxi service who were wheelchair-friendly and they agreed to come and help Mum out of the house and take her right into the hospital. Then we got in touch with the Patient Liaison Service at the hospital who agreed to meet Mum at the entrance and take her up to the ward. The only snag was that Mum didn't have a wheelchair, so that was arranged too. Robert and I went into town and brought one home. It was light in weight but durable, and this now meant that Mum could visit Dad when we were not around. Dad eventually came home and I made another trip down to see them, helping to set things up again before heading back to Scotland. I had been home only a few days, Tracy had just been released from hospital, and we had gone out for a coffee, when I had the call about Pop. It was a shock; we had expected Pop to spend many more years in the home and this news shook the whole family. Still racked by the news of Pop's death, we had to head down south again. A paramedic called me at work to say Mum had suffered a heart attack and had been rushed into hospital. Dad was on his own, so I had to get down quick to look after him. This was hard. I had to organise for Dad to be taken into care for a week or two while Mum was in hospital. I had already taken so much time off work and it was impossible to bring Dad home in his weak state. Eventually Mum was able to come home and Dad too. Again Robert and I travelled down to make the transition easy for them, and make sure they had everything they needed. We were only home a week when Mum called to say Dad had been taken back into hospital with another chest infection. At least this time Mum would be able to visit. Dad needed to have an operation, but after a while it was decided that he was too weak to go through such an invasive operation and that they would have to leave it. It was clear then that this was not a happy outcome and we made sure Mum was able to visit as much as possible. On the day Dad was due to come home, Mum had another 'turn' and ended up in hospital yet again. Dad had to go into the hospital's rehab home set in the hospital grounds. We headed down again, visiting each in turn. Dad was sleeping more and more but was always alert and so pleased to see us. "Hello Shona, hello Robert," he would say, his face lighting up, then, "how's your mam?" and, "Is she alright?" He only wanted to know that we were all okay – and he could settle again. We would walk over to see Mum and pass news from one to another. Mum wasn't well enough to go over and visit at that distance, even in a wheelchair, and Dad was bed-bound by this stage. They were there for a good few weeks and we made several journeys over that time to make sure they had everything they needed. Mum eventually came home and arrangements were made for Dad to come home too, but there was a delay in assessing what care package they would both need, so Dad had to stay for a little longer. Robert and I went down often. Then one day news came through that Dad would be coming home, but the day before he was due home, Mum was taken into hospital again and Dad's return had to be delayed once more. Robert and I travelled south once more and tried to get things sorted out. I told Dad what had happened, and that Mum was doing okay but had to stay in hospital for now. "Love you

Dad," I said, as we left. "Love you," he said. We headed home knowing that at least they were both safe and being cared for, but it was hard leaving him there. A couple of days later I had a call from the home. "Your dad's not well, his chest infection," said the Filipino nurse. Dad had been having these off and on for months now, so I asked, "Will he be ok?" "Well," she said, "he not too well." I didn't know what to do. We had just come back and I wondered whether this was just another chest infection that would clear up in a day or two. I usually put my mobile phone off at night, but for some reason kept it on. Robert and I agreed that if things weren't any better the next day we'd head down south again. The call came through at about 5 am. "Your dad's breathing has changed," the voice said. I told them we were on our way. We threw some things in a bag and headed off, praying he would pull through, and fearful of what was to happen. We had just crossed the border into England when the call came: "Your dad has passed away." Oh my God! I screamed, "No, not my dad." Tears take over, even now recalling this time. My lovely dad, gone, and I didn't have the chance to say goodbye. It's not what I ever wanted for him, to be all alone. It was heart-breaking. I phoned the hospital and asked the doctor to tell my mum. I was worried the news would be too much for her. Remarkably she received the news better than I had. I think she had prepared herself for this, but it was the saddest moment, and going in to see her after this news was so painful. Because Mum wasn't well enough to make the necessary arrangements after Dad's death, Robert and I had to, but because Dad didn't die at home or in hospital, an autopsy was called and this delayed the funeral. I had several trips to make before this could be done. Mum couldn't be at the funeral; the doctor felt it would be too much for her, so I put together a little booklet about Dad for the funeral, attended by only a handful of people, and Mum read through it in hospital at the time we were all at the crematorium. When Mum came home she was sad and lost, and it was even harder leaving her behind. "Would you like to move up with us now?" I asked her. "I'd love to," she said. There was a lot to do, and I worried that the transition would be difficult for her. I told her things would be very different in our house, it wouldn't be like her own house, and that she had to think about what she'd like to bring up with her, because we couldn't take it all. Mum was the kind of person who never threw anything out, so there was a lot of stuff. Robert and I began to make plans to convert the garage into a bedroom for her so she could either use the lounge area in the kitchen/dining room or the main lounge during the day. I was looking forward to her coming to live with us, but it wasn't going to happen overnight. There was such a lot to consider and plan. I thought we had time. Then one morning at work, I had a call from a worried neighbour. "Your mum's not well Shona," she said, "she phoned asking me to come over, she is confused and not herself, but the nurses are just arriving." She handed the phone over to my mum. "Shona, I think I've had another heart attack, but I don't think I should go into hospital." I told her to go and that I would find her, adding, "You can't go on like this Mum, we need to get you up with us soon eh?" "Yes," she said. Then I told her to go and get 'sorted out' and I would speak to her soon. It was evening before I eventually found where she was, and the hospital staff were quite bright. "Oh your mum's doing fine, we are just doing some tests, we don't think it is her heart." Relieved she was doing fine, I continued to call each day for the next few days to receive the same message. By the fourth day I was beginning to get worried. If Mum was well she would have arranged for the lady from the Patient Liaison Service to be in touch. I had a bad feeling about it and told Robert I felt I had to go down to see what was happening. Robert had meetings at work so I asked Tracy to come with me, and so we headed off. When Tracy and I got to the hospital, it was late at night. We had flown down to Stansted and caught the bus to Harlow then walked over to the hospital. I couldn't believe what met my eyes. It was clear Mum was very ill. "Did you not wonder why I wasn't here?" I asked Mum. "Yes," she whispered. "Oh Mum," I said, giving her a hug. "They told me you were fine, that's why I didn't come down, I thought you would be like you were when you were in hospital the last time!" Then I marched to the nurses' station and hit the roof! I demanded to know what was going on, asking why they had said Mum was fine when clearly she was not fine, and ended by pointing out that, living almost five-hundred miles away, I couldn't just pop in to see her and they had to let me know what was going on. Their reply was a garbled one which mentioned 'patient confidentiality' and other excuses, all of which I threw back at them. Then the young lad who had been at the receiving end of this gulped and said, "This is my first day on the ward!" Typical – I felt obliged to apologise – but not unreservedly. I demanded to speak to the doctor looking after Mum and was able to do this the following day. It turned out that Mum had suffered a urine infection, which had led to septicaemia, which she had obviously and remarkably, given her age and medical history, survived; but she was now battling 'hospital-acquired' pneumonia, the result of her lying still for too long. They had tried one course of medication which had not worked too well, and were now about to start on another. We were able to speak, but Mum was clearly very ill and she looked exhausted. She was happy to see Tracy and her spirits were lifted. We stayed only a couple of days but Robert and I returned a few days later again. By this time, Mum was less well, and when the doctor told us that she was not responding to any of the antibiotics we knew that we would lose her too. It was a reality I dared not think about, and felt absolutely desolate. Robert and I stayed with her round the clock for about three days as her breathing became shallow and difficult. Then one morning, Robert said he would pop down to the hospital's café for breakfast and I stayed with Mum. "It's just you and me now Mum," I told her. "Robert's gone for breakfast, hungry Horace." I smiled. She looked at me, trying to tell me to go too but I shook my head. "I'm not leaving you," I told her, and held her hand. She looked at me with a look in her eye that said 'sorry'. I had the dreadful sinking feeling she was asking if it was alright to go; she'd had enough. "I'll be okay Mum, Robert will look after me," I assured her, then, "I love you Mum."

"Love you too," she whispered almost silently. Then a

second or two later her face twisted as though she was in pain, and she was gone. I just laid on her and cried and cried. A minute or two later I phoned Robert but couldn't speak. He came back immediately. I hadn't even alerted hospital staff; I just wanted those last minutes to hug her and cry. I am still crying now. In many ways I was as ready as anyone can be when Dad died. I could see him fading away, and half-expected it would happen sooner rather than later, but not my mum. We had so many plans yet, so much time, I thought together. I wanted to look after her. But now she was gone, and with her a part of me went too. It was only weeks after Dad had died, it was too soon, way too soon and the grief was overwhelming. I felt like my world had come to an end.

6

LOVE, THE GREATEST
GIFT OF ALL

I have struggled since that day over the past couple of years, not just losing my Mum and Dad, but also regretting the difficult times, the teenage arguments, wilfulness, and the (too much) time we spent apart. However, this last wee while, and with the help and support of Robert and my children, my cousins and my friends, I have come to realise that there was nothing that unusual in our relationship. Robert tells me that my mum and dad were lucky to have such a caring daughter, and that I couldn't have done more for them. He said they told him how lucky they felt to have me. It reminded me of something my mum said not long before she died: "I don't deserve to have a lovely daughter like you." All this time I was thinking just the opposite, that I didn't deserve to have lovely parents like them. My mum and dad did their best. Through all the difficult times, I now realise that they were always on my side. It seems obvious now, but back then it was like we were on different sides, and fighting hard. I have beaten myself up about this for years but now I realise I was just a kid! Hearing about the exploits of some children today, and of others when I was young, I realise that I really wasn't that bad after all! I just argued and wouldn't listen to good advice, a typical teenager, some would say. As a consequence I married too young (over their dead bodies they said) and thought I'd won the battle. Looking back, I lost the battle but I did gain three brilliant children, so not all lost battles have sad endings. And I had almost forgotten that, throughout it all, I never once stopped loving my mum and dad. That's why it all hurt so much. Because in spite of it all, I loved them, always had, always will and I now realise they never stopped loving me either, despite all the arguments, tantrums, and the worry I must have given them during the teenage years,

Looking back now, it's a strange feeling recalling earlier days with a family who are no longer here anymore. It's as if I have stepped out of one life and into another. Robert and I are the grandparents now and our children will have memories very different from ours and experiences far removed from those of a life growing up in the 1960s and '70s. It brings home the fact that life is short, everyone has their own life, their own stories and with it their good times, bad times, proud moments and achievements. And everyone has moments which could best be described as 'not our finest moments', our regrets. Is this not what a full life should be, to experience all the emotions possible? I have experienced them all now and I have come to realise that no matter what we do in life, or how many times we make mistakes, we should take comfort in knowing we are not alone. 'To err is human', they say! Someone once described emotion as 'God's gift' so if this is true then the greatest gift is most certainly love. If we can give as much love as we can to those we love, then when the end of life comes to them we will eventually be able to let go, let them rest in peace, knowing that our love meant more to them than anything else in the world.

'The sands of time will never wash away
the love I have for you.'

In memory of my beloved parents,
Moira and Bill Anderson

CALENDAR OF REMEMBRANCE

February 4th

Remembering Granny Jordan this month. She was born Sophia Liddle Dobie in Edinburgh in 1904. Granny Jordan was Granddad Jordan's second wife, and my mum's stepmum. They married on 2 April 1948 when my mum had just turned sixteen. Granny Jordan had also been married before but her husband had been killed at the beginning of the war.

March 18th

I can't think of March without thinking of my lovely mum. She was born in 1932 in Edinburgh, as Moira Theresa Janet Jordan and was an only child. My mum had a tragic early life, when her mum, Janet, died aged just thirty-eight from stomach cancer in January of 1946. My mum was just two months away from her fourteenth birthday and Granddad Jordan was ill with a serious throat infection at sea, in the Royal Navy. It was just after the Second World War, so Mum had to look after herself, even at that young age, until he came home. She would take herself to the RN base at Leith, where her mum had gone to collect

Granddad's wages and with it paid the rent and all the bills for quite a few months. It couldn't have been easy. When her dad was able to come home temporarily, he arranged for her to stay with her grandparents, her mum's parents. Apparently they were reluctant to be burdened with a child and agreed to this arrangement with a heavy heart, and this began a short phase in her young life Mum recalled as 'loveless and sad', until she could be reunited with her dad a few months later.

June 2nd

Nana Anderson was born Beatrice Mary Young in 1894 in Rainton, Co Durham. I don't know when my granddad Anderson was born or anything much about him, except he died when I was about six, he was a postman, and his parents came from Hawick, although I think he was born in the Tynemouth area, or Newcastle. Nana Anderson was a lovely singer and very theatrical and starred in many amateur productions. Nana and Granddad Anderson were very mild-mannered, lovely people.

July 7th

Granddad Jordan was born William John in 1900. His parents were from County Cork in Southern Ireland and were probably migrants of the Potato Famine which cost many lives in Southern Ireland at the time, arriving in Edinburgh when Granddad Jordan was just three years old. Granddad

Jordan was one of those people who could do anything – a bit like my Robert. He was an enthusiastic gardener and loved growing vegetables in the garden and tomatoes in his greenhouse, and he always kept a beautiful garden. He made my mum's ironing board for her when she got married and she still used it until she died. Granddad Jordan had an Irish temper but with it a heart of gold.

August 22nd

Pop. Robert's dad was also called Robert Paterson and he was born on 22 August 1929 and Robert's mum Jeanie was born on 21 September 1929. Pop had been an athlete in his younger days and a good swimmer. Although I didn't know him in my younger days, Robert and I spent such a lot of time with him in his later years. Both he and Jeanie are always remembered fondly, and there will always be a special place in my heart for them both.

August 23rd

My beautiful granddaughter Kytana was born on 23 August 1996 and died on 15 February aged twelve years, the delayed result of a choking accident ten years previously, which left her severely brain-damaged. Kytana was a delightful and very much loved little girl, the daughter of my son Christopher. Her story belongs to another book, which I hope one day someone will write, to carry the family stories forward.

December 23rd

My lovely dad. An exceptional man: kind, calm, wise, gentle, and loving. He was an unforgettable man. He loved life, my mum and I, and he loved my family. Born the middle of three children, he was born simply William Anderson in Benwell, Newcastle in 1921.